Super Normal
Sensations of the Ordinary

Super Normal
Sensations
of the Ordinary

Naoto Fukasawa & Jasper Morrison

Lars Müller Publishers

Absence, ambivalence, and paradox

From a conceptual point of view there are two elements that are particularly fascinating in the Super Normal category proposed and explored by Fukasawa and Morrison: the first is that the category is based on an absence; the second is that it rests on an intentional and extraordinary ambivalence.

Absence: The Super Normal object can be defined by something that is not present. Or something it doesn't have. Style, identity, originality, remarkableness. Anything that can be seen as *excellence*, or as an unmistakably connotative brand, is incompatible with the status of the Super Normal object. Indeed, its pre-eminent quality consists in the capacity to conceal its features until they become virtually invisible. *Ambivalence:* however much we dwell on the category proposed by Fukasawa and Morrison, it is very hard to understand, fundamentally, whether Super Normal is an oxymoron (super *versus* normal) or an absolute superlative (the greatest degree of normality possible, "normality" in its ontological form, its quintessential perfection). The objects selected by Fukasawa and Morrison are, indeed, all oxymoronic and superlative: they push the norm to the boundaries of the possible and at the same time introject a sort of paradoxical *coincidentia oppositorum*. By making them so "normal" they aren't normal any more, they become both "normal" and "exceptional" at the same time. So exceptional they seem normal. In other words, they are not perceived or perceivable as exceptional. At least, that is, until they are noticed and co-opted by the *auctoritas* of Morrison and Fukasawa. It is only at this point that the Super Normal object reveals the paradox embedded in its genetic code: at the very instant it is perceived, catalogued, and exhibited as such, Super Normal transcends itself.

Silvana Annicchiarico

Design Curator
La Triennale di Milano

Translation: Lucinda Byatt

The Visualizers

"They said I'd never make it to Normal. They were wrong."
Bob Dylan at a concert in Normal, Illinois, 1999.

One thing is certain: with their "Super Normal" project Jasper
Morrison and Naoto Fukasawa are treading uncertain ground.
Neither the normal nor Super Normal can claim to be clearly
demarcated concepts in terms of any scientific conventions.
Although the etymology of normal relates it to the norm
and the normative, our ideas of normality, of normal things and
processes, are anything but normalized. Yet precisely the
fuzziness of the concept is what Morrison and Fukasawa exploit
in their eponymous exhibitions in Tokyo and London, and
in this book as well. Here each of the everyday objects they
recognize as Super Normal becomes evidence, testifying
to thoughtful and deliberate design beyond pathos and the
modernistic masquerade: A paper clip. A plastic bucket.
A chair. The two designers have rounded up some 200 objects,
presenting them on white blocks and steles. As such, each
exhibit achieves maximum effect in shape, color and materiality
while also entering into a dialogue with all the other things
united in the exhibition. Naoto Fukasawa: "Surprisingly there
was not a single collision in our opinions. We talked primarily about
what to include in the exhibition, or not, in order to make the
idea of Super Normal more understandable to general audiences."

In this exhibition an affinity becomes apparent between what
is Super Normal and what has become archetypal as the result
of a long design process. The history of a product, lasting anywhere
from a century to a millennium, ultimately leads to the genesis
of an object that conjures the picture we all see in our minds when
we hear or read the word "chair," for instance. Morrison's Plywood
Chair of 1988, produced by Vitra, certainly comes quite close
to the archetype of a chair. But a closer look reveals differences:
the gentle sway of the backrest; the intentional flaunting of the
simple, flattened Phillips head screw; the surprising lightness of the
chair; and not least the exceptional simplicity of its construction,
which is clearly evident on the underside of the seat. Such properties distinguish this chair from a merely archetypal seating object,
a quasi three-dimensional pictogram. The same is true of Naoto
Fukasawa's "Déjà-vu" stool for Magis, whose form and proportions
seem to be of almost rustic plainness. Here, too, it is the selected
material, in this case aluminum, and the resulting reflections
and lightness, that distinguish the stool. This stool spontaneously
reminded me of Jeff Koons' *Rabbit,* in which the American artist
transformed an inflatable toy bunny into a chrome-plated sculpture.
Fukasawa, too, converts an existing form, conventionally associated

exclusively with a certain material (wood), into a Super Normal object, through his idiosyncratic choice of a new, unconventional material. And this is where the difference between the normal and Super Normal product becomes apparent: Super Normal refers to the normal – in the sense of adopting a familiar form and aesthetic – without being "normal" itself and merely availing itself of traditional shapes, materials or production techniques. It is precisely the conscious distance the Super Normal object maintains from its precursors that can become a subtle signal. The shape of Morrison's electric kettle for Rowenta, for instance, resembles an electrified jug – we recognize it instantly from everyday encounters with jugs or from Morandi's still lifes; we can operate it intuitively, and its grace coupled with super normality even manages to compensate for its technical deficiencies. (Rowenta's production was so shoddy that neither the process of turning it on nor the automatic shut off were as efficient as in much uglier specimens of this product type!)

The traditional sign repertoire of both Western and Asian design, we learn from this project, can become the signpost for contemporary and future generations of designers, but only if they are not under the sway of the superficial adaptation of formalities. All this has nothing to do with retrogressive design. Rather, Jasper Morrison speaks openly of the "loss of innocence" separating today's designers from the craftsmen and artisans of previous centuries. They manufactured objects for everyday use – a ladle, an axe, a saddle – without seeking to express themselves or their age, or even to hold their ground against the products of the competition or forgeries. Yet Morrison and Fukasawa work for many large, international companies, without whose production and distribution facilities no industrial design would be conceivable. There is no question that these two designers are conscious of contemporary market mechanisms, marketing strategies and production conditions. Not even Super Normal design can take place in an ivory tower, or abandon itself to sentimentalities. It has to take the market into account in order to make an impact. But instead of resorting to cheap tricks or exalted gestures, that impact can only be achieved through sophisticated forms and details that clearly reveal the fruitful legacy of traditions and progenitors in design history.

In addition to anonymous design, such as the Swiss Rex peeler or a simple plastic bag, the collection includes design classics like Max Bill's wall clock for Junghans, the 606 shelving system by Dieter Rams, or Colombo's Optic alarm clock of 1970. With products by Newson, Grcic, Van Severen or the Bouroullec brothers, Morrison and Fukasawa also present the work of their own generation. Thus the selection does not simply celebrate "ordinary design," which engineers are so fond of organizing; it does not romanticize a certain decade of design or an idiom that typifies the products of a given country–and it does not focus on mere topicality, exclusivity, or the costliness of the products. The phenomenon of Super Normal is therefore placed outside time and space; both the past and the present of product design point in equal measure to a future that has long since begun. Quite obviously, the two men are not concerned with studies and utopian models: Super Normal is already there, out in the open; it exists in the here and now; it is real and available. We have only to open our eyes: Fukasawa and Morrison visualize it for us.

Almost exactly thirty years before the first Super Normal exhibition in the Axis Gallery in Tokyo, *Das gewöhnliche Design* (Ordinary Design) exhibition took place at the Mathildenhöhe in Darmstadt, a center of German Jugendstil. At that time Friedrich Friedl and Gerd Ohlhauser presented bicycle tires, dowels, pocket tissues, bottle openers, file folders, and clothespins in the rooms of that city's Fachhochschule für Design. West German household wares of the seventies were declared to be objects of study. In his talk at the opening of the exhibition, Bazon Brock, Professor for Aesthetics in Wuppertal, said, "We must analyze and understand our contemporary everyday world as if it were the everyday world of a historical society. For example, the everyday world of Pompeii at the time of 79 B.C., when Vesuvius buried the city once and for all, thus preserving it for us." Explicitly selected to counteract the dominant role and overly solemn approach to Jugendstil in Darmstadt at the time, the 110 objects seem, at first glance, to prefigure the Super Normal project. However, closer observation reveals a different focus, namely, on the banality of the object world. There was hardly a single product in the collection that cost more than three to five Deutschmarks: with considerable wit and finesse, bathtub stoppers, paper plates, pencils, and beer bottles in display cases were set against the florally ornamentalized, precious Jugendstil furniture and lamps with their flowing forms and exalted gestures. Hence, location and date–Darmstadt, 1976–played a decisive role in the exhibition, while the presentation of Super Normal by Fukasawa and Morrison carries the same message and force of expression in any country of the Western world by highlighting a subject matter that is as long-lasting as many of the selected products.

So why is the visualization of Super Normal necessary just now? To answer this, it is enough to visit a couple of department stores, supermarkets, trade fairs, and websites or to take a quick glance at lifestyle magazines and coffee table books. Everything that is superficially spectacular and pseudo-modern has long since become normality in product design: superfluous features, ellipses, dynamic curvatures, perforations, and pearlescent paint dominate today's styling. This applies equally to most cars (inside and out) as well as sports articles, stereos, clocks, and furniture – not to mention packaging design. In contrast, a few years ago Fukasawa designed a fluorescent yellow, upright container for banana juice with slightly browned edges reminiscent of the banana itself, but without imitating its typical bend. Its spout is even opened with the same hand movement used to peel a banana. Wouldn't it be super if such design one day became normal?

Gerrit Terstiege

Gerrit Terstiege is editor-in-chief of the design journal *form*. He was a lecturer at the academies of design in Karlsruhe, Basel and Zurich, and a visiting professor for design and media history at the Mainz University of Applied Sciences. In addition he is a board member of the Deutsche Gesellschaft für Designtheorie und -forschung. www.form.de, www.dgtf.de

Translation: Susan E. Richter

1 Wastepaper basket
A cylinder is the most normal form that a wastepaper basket takes. With a slight tilt in the direction in which people toss their garbage, this wastepaper basket has become a new normal. The lip of the wastepaper basket being slightly thicker makes it easier to carry. Generally with molded plastic goods, attempts are made to keep the thickness of the plastic as uniform as possible to create a smooth surface. If there is a thicker section in a uniform material, a dent may appear as the material hardens, since the temperature doesn't drop uniformly through the material. This is called a "dimple defect," and it is usual for molded goods with many of these dimples to be considered poor quality. But with this wastepaper basket, it has been possible to achieve such a dimple the entire way around the lip of the wastepaper basket mouth, so that it is thicker than the rest of the body.

It is not easy to revamp something normal, making it easier to use and thus creating a new normal. This wastepaper basket has succeeded in generating a normal that surpasses normal by using a technical factor, generally considered to be negative, to positive effect.

2 Wooden chair
A chair with a squarish seat and cylindrical legs was a common
theme in the 1970s, but always done in an uncompromisingly
modern way, with no gesture to the body or reminder of the past.
This one goes further, and in the gentle curve of the back legs
we sense a tradition, older than the first Thonet chair, of the kind
of comfort that is suggested by the relaxed lines of its structure.
It's modern enough not to be concerned with being modern.

3 Citrus basket
You'd imagine this fruit basket (present in almost every bar
in Italy) had been designed by Sottsass in the 1970s, but in fact
it was designed by the Alessi technical office in 1952. It probably
takes inspiration from a tradition of more finely wired bread-
baskets, which were made much earlier. Increasing the scale
of the wire and adjusting the proportions to suit a new function
make this object genuinely Super Normal.

4 Barbecue
This is the standard for barbecue grills. You feel like you can smell the meat grilling just by looking at the shape. The "sizzle effect" is something that whets the appetite and tempts the taste buds. It's similar to the sound of beer being poured into a glass, of juice being squeezed, of meat cooking, or the sight of steam coming off hot food. The effect of shape along with taste and feel means that it is so standardized as to have become a normal that surpasses normal. Friday night – you can just smell the wonderful aromas emanating from the small balcony this grill makes its home on.

In April 2005, a series of aluminium stools I designed for Magis was shown at the Salone del Mobile in Milan. When I went to see the display at the trade fair, in contrast to other exhibits drawing attention under the spotlights, I found my three stools placed in a corner of the booth serving as rest seats for tired exhibition-goers. People probably didn't even think they were design pieces. I must admit I was a bit shocked by this, and a little depressed. Of course I'd designed stools that anyone might normally use in different situations, and was also hoping that they would prove popular with many different customers, so the fact that people went ahead and sat on them instead of viewing them as exhibited objects was, in a sense, perfectly in keeping with that aim. Or so I tried to convince myself, though it was hard to take an enlightened view of things at such a showcase venue. That evening, however, Jasper Morrison called to tell me he'd seen my stools. Here I'd been feeling dejected, yet he was enthusing like a child who's discovered some new treat: "That's Super Normal!" Apparently, he'd gone around the fair together with Takashi Okutani, who inadvertently said something to that effect when he saw my stools. Jasper seized upon the word as exactly the right conceptual handle for the appeal he'd long cherished in things "ordinary."

Designers generally do not think to design the "ordinary." If anything, they live in fear of people saying their designs are "nothing special." Of course, undeniably, people do have an unconscious everyday sense of "normal," but rather than try to blend in, the tendency for designers is to try to create "statement" or "stimulation." So "normal" has come to mean "unstimulating" or "boring" design.

It's not just designers; people who buy design and clients who commission designers do not see "normal" as a design concept or even entertain the idea of creating a "new normal." To dare, then, to design something "normal" within this prevailing scheme of design common sense raises the stakes; it makes for a consciously designed normal above-and-beyond normal that what we might call "Super Normal." Why super? Well, if our sense of normal falls within the realm of non-design, then the unthinkable attempt to undercut all the excesses and bold, brash statements recognised as design must conversely transcend them. "Normal" refers to things as they've come to be; thus "Super Normal" is the designing of things just as "normal" as what we've come to know, albeit in no way anonymous. There's a creative intent at work here, even if that intent may be regarded not so much as designing, but simply not going against the inevitable flow of things as they come to be.

"Super Normal" is less concerned with designing beauty than seemingly homely but memorable elements of everyday life. Certainly nothing "flash" or "eye-catching"; never contrived, but rather almost "naff" yet somehow appealing. As if, when viewing something with expectations of a new design, our negative first impressions of "nothing much" or "just plain ordinary" shifted to "…but not bad at all." Overcoming an initial emotional denial, our bodily sensors pick up on an appeal we seem to have known all along and engage us in that strangely familiar attraction. Things that possess a quality to shake us back to our senses are "Super Normal."

When people hear the word "design," they think "special"; creating "special" things is what everyone, designers and users alike, assume design is all about. When in fact, both sides are playing out a mutal fantasy far removed from real life.

I'd like us to explore whatever we might conceive as Super Normal. I take an interest in collecting such things. I want to share the fun, the pleasure of reconfirming an appeal in things we'd disregarded as "naff." Not that I propose sticking "Certified Super Normal" product design award labels on things. It's much more of a quietly seen unseen, a refreshing surprise that awakens the person who had thought of looking for something obviously special in design by instead reconfirming what we already hold important and so perhaps letting us break free of our current design paradigm straitjacket.

When I'm true to my feelings, I really "get" Super Normal.

Naoto Fukasawa

Translation: Alfred Birnbaum

5 Air filter
This air filter is shaped like the louvers of air ducts
that you often find installed in walls. Since louvers are
symbolic of the passage that air takes, it would perhaps
feel as if the air really was being cleaned before your eyes
if this louver-shaped air filter was placed in a room and
drew in something visible like cigarette smoke before you.
The passage that air takes has its own fixed shape. It may
seem that making the air filter the shape of the louvers
found in the air passage–rather than creating some kind
of new shape–is extremely normal, but that is not the
general opinion. That's why this is a Super Normal air filter.

6 Square brush washer
This is a ceramic brush washer. The inner thickness is uniform,
while all of the outer corners have a uniform R (radius). Its function
defines the rectangular shape created by the two wells, which
hold just the right amount of water for their intended purpose.
The soft shape contradicts the precision of ceramic and has
a warm feel to it. If a shape that follows function is too functional,
its relationship to people may turn cold. By maintaining a gentle
relationship with people, there's no doubt that this receptacle
has become something Super Normal.

I was having a cup of tea with Takashi Okutani in Milan, during the 2005 Salone del Mobile, talking about projects underway with Muji and describing to him the Alessi cutlery project and how I was feeling this approach to design, of leaving out the design, seemed more and more the way to go.

I mentioned having seen Naoto Fukasawa's aluminium stools for Magis and how they seemed to have a special kind of normality about them, and he added: "super normal". That was it, a name for what's been going on, a perfect summary of what design should be, now more than ever.

A while ago I found some heavy old hand-blown wine glasses in a junk shop. At first it was just their shape which attracted my attention, but slowly, using them every day, they have become something more than just nice shapes, and I notice their presence in other ways. If I use a different type of glass, for example, I feel something missing in the atmosphere of the table. When I use them the atmosphere returns, and each sip of wine's a pleasure even if the wine is not. If I even catch a look at them on the shelf they radiate something good. This quota of atmospheric spirit is the most mysterious and elusive quality in objects. How can it be that so many designs fail to have any real beneficial effect on the atmosphere, and yet these glasses, made without much design thought or any attempt to achieve anything other than a good ordinary wine glass, happen to be successful? It's been puzzling me for years and influencing my attitude to what constitutes a good design. I've started to measure my own designs against objects like these glasses, and not to care if the designs become less noticeable. In fact a certain lack of noticeability has become a requirement.

Meanwhile design, which used to be almost unknown as a profession, has become a major source of pollution. Encouraged by glossy lifestyle magazines, and marketing departments, it's become a competition to make things as noticeable as possible by means of colour, shape and surprise. It's historic and idealistic purpose, to serve industry and the happy consuming masses at the same time, of conceiving things easier to make and better to live with, seems to have been side-tracked. The virus has already infected the everyday environment. The need for businesses to attract attention provides the perfect carrier for the disease. Design makes things seem special, and who wants normal if they can have special? And that's the problem. What has grown naturally and unselfconsciously over the years cannot easily be replaced. The normality of a street of shops which has developed over time, offering various products and trades, is a delicate organism. Not that old things shouldn't be replaced or that new things are bad, just that things which are designed to attract attention are usually unsatisfactory. There are better ways to design than putting a big effort into making something look special. Special is generally less useful than normal, and less rewarding in the long term. Special things demand attention for the wrong reasons, interrupting potentially good atmosphere with their awkward presence.

The wine glasses are a signpost to somewhere beyond normal, because they transcend normality. There's nothing wrong with normal of course, but normal was the product of an earlier, less self conscious age, and designers working at replacing old with new and hopefully better, are doing it without the benefit of innocence which normal demands. The wine glasses and other objects from the past reveal the existence of Super Normal, like spraying paint on a ghost. You may have a feeling it's there but it's difficult to see. The Super Normal object is the result of a long tradition of evolutionary advancement in the shape of everyday things, not attempting to break with the history of form but rather trying to summarise it, knowing its place in the society of things. Super Normal is the artificial replacement for normal, which with time and understanding may become grafted to everyday life.

Jasper Morrison

7 Bathroom stool
In Japan, where washing takes place sitting on low stools,
this one represents a good summary of the modern typology
of variations in plastic. The exaggerated radius of the foot
in no way detracts from the smoothness of the form, which
is as easy on the eye as it is on the behind.

8 Bucket
Available all over Italy from north to south, but mysteriously
never exported, this bucket with molded pouring spout and easy
carrying handle represents the summit of bucket design and,
at a cost of about €1.50, is a perfect example of how design can
make life better for everyone.

9 Shopping Basket
This is the most common shape for a supermarket shopping
basket. This basket, created using plastic just thick enough
to withstand the weight it must bear, is perfect for a plastic molded
object in terms of function. In addition, every hole in the basket
has an R (radius) to it; there are no sharp burrs that may
hurt the user's hands. Copied in plastic from baskets originally
made of woven bamboo or knitted string, they impart a sense
of phoniness that has surpassed the original and become
a functionally excellent "normal." A copy turning into the real
thing is Super Normal.

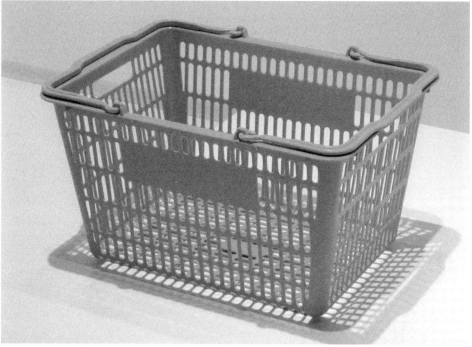

10 Bicycle
It's on the small side, while having the most "bicycle-like"
proportions. As many superfluous parts as possible have been
eliminated; but it's not as cool or as serious as a sports bicycle.
It's a "bicycle-like" bicycle, suited to taking a ride around
one's neighborhood.

11 Kitchen chair
Kitchen chairs probably started looking like this around the
end of the 1940s. With this one Enzo Mari has precisely summarized
the whole typology, tidying up all the unresolved issues both
visually and technically. There need never be another kitchen stool,
although there probably will be. Super Normal can represent
a kind of end game in design, beyond which point things can
only go downhill. It's a bit like the racing bicycle which could be
considered to have reached its peak around 1985, after which
the improvements may have performance benefits but the object
itself suffers an identity crisis.

12 Ashtray
There are no grooves to hold cigarettes in this ashtray, which
has been fashioned from heat resistant hard resin. It looks like
nothing but an ashtray, even though the details that define an
ashtray are not there. Things like the sense of volume expressed
by the plastic and the lackadaisical vividness of the red color
create the "ashtray" feel of this.

13 Uni-tray
This tray, one of Riki Watanabe's representative works, is most
often used next to a cash register as something on which to place
a customer's change. The surface of the tray is gently curved
towards the edges, making it easy to grasp coins with four fingers.
Some people use it as a pen tray; others use it to keep their
accessories and other bits and pieces on. This versatility means
that there is a great deal of freedom attached to its use, and
this extended use makes it Super Normal.

14 Canary sandals

This is a "fake" sandal formed from a single molded piece of rubber; the pattern has been taken from a standard, upscale leather women's sandal. Japanese people, who do not wear their shoes in the home and who don't want to go to the trouble of putting shoes on when they're stepping outside for just a short time, wear this kind of sandal. They are often used in public toilets, too. The most common color is a light brown, really an unappealing color, but these are green—perhaps an attempt to be a little more fashionable? These copies of fashionable sandals are as unfashionable as can be but there is no sandal more sandal-like than this. And they're water resistant and easy to wear. When I saw professional surfers in Okinawa and people working at the beach wearing the green ones, they strangely fit in with their deeply tanned bodies and looked really good—like local pros, rather than surfers wearing flip flops just to look good.

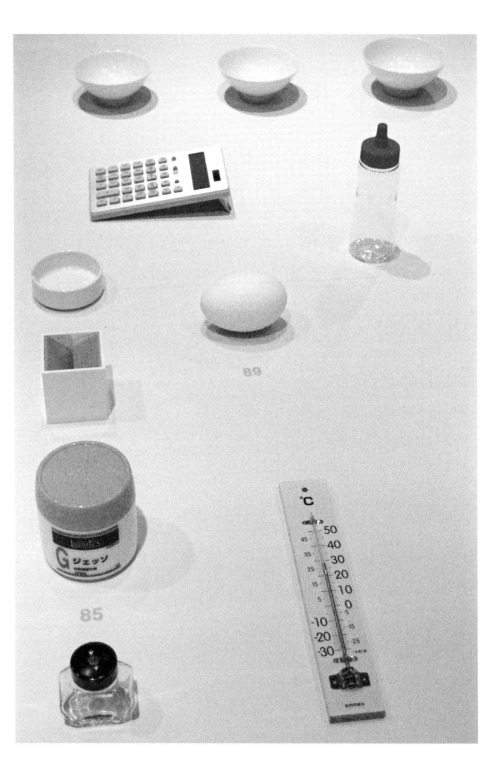

15 Goose egg
The goose egg illustrates a Super Normal device very nicely,
namely, by shifting the conventional scale or proportion of objects,
they acquire Super Normal properties. Seeing the goose egg
we are not surprised by the form at all, but the scale of it warps
our perception momentarily, allowing us to see somethingnormal
in a new way. There's nothing wrong with the form a chicken
egg except that we are used to seeing it, but seeing the goose
egg we can enjoy the form as if seeing it for the first time.

16 Calculator
The same shift of scale works for this calculator, the design of
which was based on a normal pocket type model, scaled up to make
it a desk model. The increased size of it makes it comfortable
to use, and we perceive it with amusement as its size momentarily
gives us the feeling that the world just got bigger.

17 Ashtray
At first glance, just a normal ashtray, but having only one slot
for the cigarette, it becomes an ashtray for one, or an ashtray with
a new dynamic in use. One person gets to use the slot and others
don't. You might say that's a functional deficiency, but it could make
for a more interesting and lively experience. Imagine three people
smoking, one of them subconsciously satisfied with the situation
and two uncomfortable about something but not sure what.

89

106

BIALETTI

107

18 Bottle opener
The old bottle opener we are familiar with is here wrapped in
a plastic molding, exposed at the functional end and comfortable
at the holding end. We perceive the old bottle opener subconsciously and yet we appreciate the newness of the object. It is both
comfortingly normal and surprisingly unexpected.

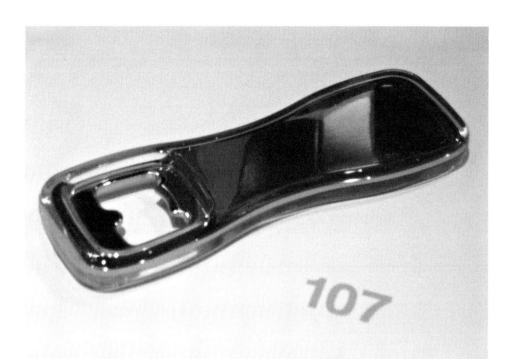

107

19 Stools
Like the bottle opener on the previous page these stools
are both old and new. The typology is one we are well used to,
nothing spectacular but satisfying all the same, but switching
the materials allows us to appreciate the object in a new light,
and suppressing its formal aspects allows us to appreciate
it for what it is.

20 Cocktail shaker
The basic form of the shaker is in keeping with the
language of most cocktail shakers, but the addition of two
dents, which help both to keep a grip on it while shaking
and to facilitate its opening, distinguish it as Super Normal.

21 Plastic sieve

Originally, a sieve made of fine woven strips of bamboo
was used to drain water off cut vegetables or rinse
boiled noodles in cold water, but plastic, which is more
functional in terms of deterioration and rough handling,
is now the standard. Bamboo sieves are very attractive
and go well with the foodstuffs that are washed in them,
but strangely the ugly imitation coupled with the foodstuffs
has come to look tasty.

The mouthwatering atmosphere exuded by a shabby
shop whose strength lies in the flavor of its food is conjured
by this new standard sieve.

22 Ice bucket
The ice bucket belongs to the same family as the cocktail
shaker; the family resemblance lies in the gentle tapering
of the shape and in the repeat of the two dents, which in this
case serve as handles when lifting what would otherwise
be a heavy and slippery object.

23 Fiber-tipped pen
The most popular fiber-tipped pen, unchanging over time.
A cross-section shows a gentle hexagonal shape. The thickness
of the pen feels good in the hand, and it is easy to write with.
Of all the pens randomly tossed into a drawer, this is the one
that we inevitably reach for. Usually black or red, but every now
and then you may come across grey, green and orange ones,
too. For an old standard item with a shape people have a soft
spot for, these colors are very fresh and appear to
surpass normal.

24 Package-carrier handle
This simple handle is passed through the strings wrapped
around a heavy cardboard box to prevent the string
from cutting into the carrier's hand. When considering how
to create a handle that's the easiest to grasp while minimizing
production costs and using the least amount of material
possible, any thoughts or ambitions with respect to design
vanish into thin air. One focuses only on the functionality
that will satisfy these difficult conditions. The result is an
anonymous shape, the ultimate in minimal, that has
come to be called normal.

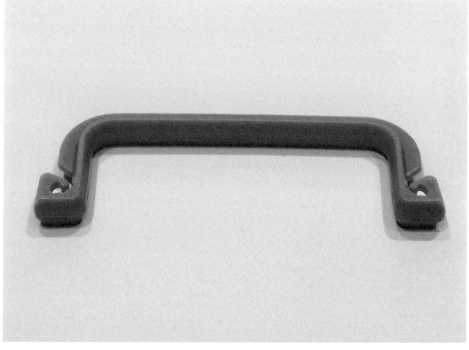

25 Waste bin
The tapering shape expresses an enthusiasm to receive
trash, like most waste bins do. In this case, though, the addition
of a lid with a hole goes a step further by offering to keep its
contents hidden. A ring inside discreetly supports the plastic bag.

26 Table
A table, looking like what anyone might draw – four legs, one at
each corner, straight and square and nothing unexpected except
the thinness of the top, which defies our expectations of what
would be strong enough to do the job. So the table becomes a live
presence in a way that other tables do not. A high performance
super-table.

27 Coat stand
Delivered in a tube, this miraculous structure is erected in
seconds, braced by its extra level that provides 3 extra hanging
points at its ends and 3 hooks where it meets the lower structure.
The unfolding of the elements creates a light but stable structure
with such ease of purpose and elegance that to see it is to
appreciate the character of a good coat stand. Super without
trying to be special.

28 Sake glass

The summary of all Sake glasses, the cup-shaped cup held off the table by a weighted base-shaped base, both made for each other. The shape comes from a classic Japanese ceramic or lacquerware bowl typology, while the deformation and change of material make for the most natural vessel imaginable for the precious liquid.

29 Soy sauce dispenser

This soy sauce dispenser designed by Masahiro Mori has such an iconic presence that it automatically comes to mind when we think of soy sauce. In fact, its presence even overlaps with, say, the presence of a good sushi shop. Going to a good sushi shop and finding a different soy sauce dispenser would perhaps make you feel like something just wasn't right. "Normal" is something that is created through the existence of an object interlaced with the overall atmosphere that surrounds it.

30 Table salt shaker
In days gone by, the general store on the street corner
was called a tobacco shop, and salt was always sold there
along with cigarettes. This table salt shaker is one that
seems to hark back to that time. Since then, salt has been
revamped, with a new bottle making the scene. But when
you get down to it, this stable conical shape is still an icon
for table salt. Many shakers, whether by coincidence or not,
have the same kind of shape. What they share is that, while
having a functional shape, they also have a gentleness,
a softness about them.

31/32 Pepper mill and sugar sifter
Hard to imagine a more perfect industrial object, or a better
pepper mill, the perfect blend of industrial technique, refined
function and charming companion at the table. The sugar sifter
must have been a natural next step, making use of the same
black plastic base to close the open-ended conical body.

33 Paper clip
Tiny balls added to the ends of what is otherwise a normal
paper clip make the difference between scratched and not
scratched pages when applying the clip. They also change the
whole experience of clipping paper together, being much easier
on the fingers and having a certain extra quality about them.

34 Digital camera
The relatively large handle section makes it easy to operate
the camera with one hand. It is a compact camera that originally
took film and has now been digitalized without changing the
traditional style at all. Equipped with an interchangeable
lens function, high image quality, and high pixel count, it easily
competes with the functions of a professional single-lens reflex
camera. The combination of unchanging normal shape and
super-enhanced performance makes this camera Super Normal.

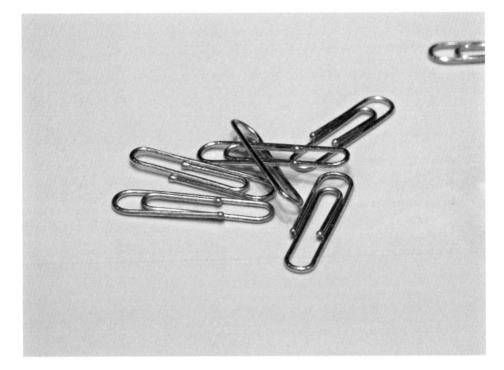

35 Cutter

Cutter, the generic name for the type of knife where one pushes up the blade to snap off the end that has become dull, stems from this NT cutter. Ivory plastic covers the outside of the metal guide that encases the blade. Despite its slim line, the cutter is shaped to allow an easy grip. When searching for things that were Super Normal, this was not the cutter that sprang to mind, but rather the slimmest, simplest form where the protective plastic part was removed to reveal the metal guide. And when I went to a stationery shop to buy it, I realized that the NT cutter lying next to it, which had been around for years, was Super Normal. It is still the easiest to use and appears to be something people have a soft spot for. It was not nostalgia I felt but rather the feeling that I was looking at the essence of a cutter.

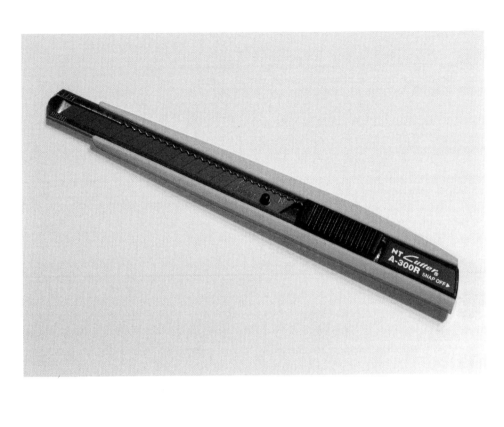

36 Tea cup
Part of a set of tableware recently designed by the late
Masahiro Mori for Muji. The exterior is smooth white porcelain,
while the interior makes use of a very slight radial ridging that
appears like textured pattern when glazed. The ridging is so
slight that the texture can be seen more than felt, and the contrast
between outside and inside surfaces adds a certain richness
to what might otherwise be an ordinary tea cup. Porcelain is cheap
these days but it should be remembered that it was once more
valued than gold, and it remains a remarkable and unrivalled
material for tableware.

37 Ice cream spoon
A masterpiece of manipulation of a thin sheet of stainless steel.
The curves are so subtle and so carefully considered for the hand
and the eye that the spoon appears to have volume. Sori Yanagi's
attention to detail in this case results in the seemingly impossible
conjuring trick of making the 2-dimensional seem 3-dimensional.

38 Thermometer
When I first learned what a thermometer was for in my elementary
school cooking class, it looked like this one. A glass rod fixed
to a wooden board with clear-cut numbers: a visual image of that
elusive thing called "temperature." Even the introduction of digital
devices cannot detract from the fact that this thermometer attached
to a wooden mount is an icon.

39 Flour scoop
A process similar to the ice cream spoon, but more complicated,
is used to make this scoop. The manipulating of a flat sheet
of stainless steel in this case results in a far less subtle and yet
undeniably effective shape. The scoop has all the characteristics
to qualify it as 100% adequate for its purpose. The rounded ends
allowing easy access to the bag, and the angle between handle and
blade is just right for the job. The object is so relaxed and natural
in appearance that it overcomes its own ordinariness.

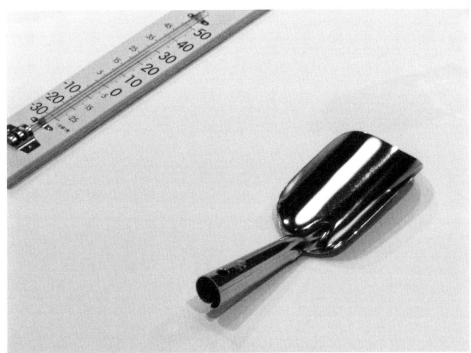

40 Bowl and sieve

A traditional idea revisited and perfected by Sori Yanagi.
The sieve fits inside the bowl, its rim slightly overlapping the rim
of the bowl for easy lifting and straining of vegetables or noodles
or whatever else needs rinsing and straining. When Yanagi
visited the Tokyo exhibition he commented on several exhibits.
"This is beautiful", "What's that for?" and so on, and when
he came to these bowls, he asked admiringly "Who designed
these?" That is surely the greatest testament to his ability
to design things so natural that they become one with the world
of objects rather than remaining aloof as design masterpieces.

41/42 Vermilion Calligraphy ink and "Yamato" library paste bottle
School supplies: one container holds the red ink used in
calligraphy; the other holds glue. The contents are completely
different, but they are both poured into blow-molded soft PP
containers. The containers have a gentleness, a softness
not found in similar items for professional use. When the user
is a child, when it is an educational material, or when it is
for beginners, the shape of an object is gentle and easy
to understand. Since everyone uses the same thing at school,
it becomes something normal to everyone.

43 Salt/cocoa castor
Well within the everyday language of these types of object
and yet generously over-proportioned for the job, they become
the professional choice for the kitchen.

44 Bar sugar bowl
Like the citrus basket, this sugar bowl can be found on almost
every bar in Italy and represents the highest level of sophistication
in design. It makes use of a basic material (stainless steel) and
the available industrial processes to give shape to an object that
serves its purpose perfectly in every way. It's easy and interesting
to use, the cut-aways allow two spoons to be positioned for
comfortable access, while the rim of the lid folds outwards at the
front to provide an easy lifting point. Normally, incorporating all
of these features in one material might easily lead to an unshapely
and awkward result but here everything works together and
the result is as graceful as a sugar bowl could ever hope to be.

45 Grill pan
Another Sori Yanagi design which refines a traditional kitchen
item by finding beautiful and natural form to match its function.
Yanagi's method involves a lot of hand modeling before the
final shape is defined on paper, while we all use computers and
3-d drawing programs. Looking at an object like this one reminds
us of what we may be sacrificing in the name of efficiency.

46 Milk bottle

Milk used to be delivered to the doorstep early in the morning. Like newspapers. The shape of this milk bottle hasn't changed since then. The bottles are used over and over again so the glass is thick to keep them from breaking easily. The delicious flavor of milk overlaps with the shape of this bottle. It is a friendly shape with no feel of precision to it and the most normal shape for milk.

47 Tumbler

Cafés, soba shops, and casual restaurants use glasses that
can be stacked. These tumblers are especially for drinking water
or iced tea and almost nobody uses them at home. They came
to mind when I was thinking about the definition of Super Normal.
What would you think, for example, if you were invited to a
friend's house and were served iced tea or water in one of these
glasses? You'd probably wonder why your friend was using
them because it's perhaps more normal to give a guest in your
home a glass that is a little better in terms of design. The circumstances under which water is drunk from this glass are fixed.
Having quickly finished your meal at, say, a soba shop where you
eat standing up, you drain the glass in one gulp. This is probably
a shared feeling of the most refreshing way to drink water.
When this ordinary feeling finds its way into the home, it seems
strange. But perhaps your friend wanted especially to offer
you this normal "refreshing-way-to-drink-water" feeling. Perhaps
there is a more generous serving of love in this normal feeling
than if you had been served something in a glass chosen for its
design. The appeal of Super Normal lies in the idea that our
relationship with things we aren't usually aware of is richer than
with things that are viewed in terms of design.

48 Wineglass
A simple stemmed wineglass, probably around 100 years old,
probably made for a French bar. It's the absolute opposite of all
the special ones on the market today, wine glasses that want
us to believe they are essential for enjoying specific types of wine.
They're the kind of glasses that spoil the atmosphere of a dinner
table faster than a bowl of foul tasting soup! A basic form like this
one, with its unassuming nature, has all the character to make
almost any wine taste good, and even with the last drop emptied,
it still continues to give good atmosphere to the table.

49 Door handle

The shape of this door handle is taken from an old coach handle,
the type of coach pulled by horses before cars became the norm.
The form of the original handle had a character about it that
seemed to be the essence of all handles, a kind of distillation
of what you'd expect a handle to look like.

50 Vegetable peeler

A classic example of achieving the most with the least. Nothing
showy about this implement, but once held in the hand and tested
on a potato or a carrot, there's no mistaking its efficiency or the
beauty of thought behind it.

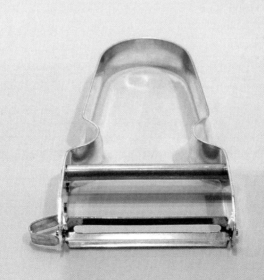

51 Spanners

These forged spanners make no claim to be anything
but adequate for their purpose, and yet in the directness
of the detailing and the peculiar poetry of their formal
composition, they succeed in surpassing their ordinary status.

52 Felt undershoes

This item of footwear is made to be worn inside rubber boots
as an insulating sock, but seen out of their boots they seem
to represent the history of all footwear. They are more like
the essence of Super Normalness than an actual Super Normal
object. Given how flat felt sheet behaves, they seem to defy
the possibility of their own manufacture.

Francesca Picchi: Super Normal has been received as a kind of manifesto of what design should be according to you. Today there is a certain ambiguity about the term design (about its meaning); generally it is perceived as something to "make nicer things." Can Super Normal be considered as a sort of theory? Or an attempt at theorizing what good design is or should be?

Naoto Fukasawa: Super Normal is not a theory. I believe it's re-realizing something that you already knew, re-acknowledging what you naturally thought was good in something. It's true that design is all about improving what already exists, but there's also the danger that things that were already good get changed. Design is expected to provide something "new" or "beautiful" or "special." When we look at the things around us with such a mindset, those things outside "design" are viewed as being "normal" or "ugly" in contrast. Super Normal consists of the things that we overlook when we focus too much on "design"—I think it points to those things in our everyday lives that we naturally hold an affinity for. I believe Super Normal is the inevitable form that results from the lengthy use of a thing—shall we say, a core of awareness. Design is refining that "normal" core existence bit by bit so that it fits in with our lives today. Then this exceeds normal and becomes Super Normal. Those things that never change can also be called Super Normal. I think that Super Normal indicates our "realization" of what is good in "normal."

Jasper Morrison: I don't mind the definition to "make nicer things." If design achieved this occasionally, it would be fine! I agree Super Normal isn't a theory, it's more of a "noticing". Super Normal has been around for a long time, probably since the first pots were made. It's an aspect of how we live with and relate to objects rather than a system for designing better things, although I think there's a lot to be learnt from that. Objects become Super Normal through use rather than design, although their design is a key factor. You might not know something was Super Normal simply by looking at it, nor would you know it by using it once. It's more of a long-term discovery of the quality of an object, which goes beyond the initial visual judgment and basic assessment that we make of things when we first notice them. Super Normal may belong more to everyday life than it does to design.

FP: What could be a possible definition of Super Normal?

NF: It refers to something that already exists, something so ordinary or normal that everybody points to it and says, "That's really normal!" It can also mean something that has been newly designed, which people look at with the expectation of being blown away by its newness or by something special about it. Instead they say, "Huh?! That's just so…normal!" So it's something that packs a surprise at odds with our expectations.

JM: An even more basic definition could be something that's good to have around, that you use in a completely satisfactory way without having to think about its shape or decipher any hidden message or trickiness. If you went into a shop looking for a dining plate, it would be the most plate-like plate you could find. Even more plate-like than you could imagine a plate to be. What's good about a more than plate-like plate is that it will do its job without messing up the atmosphere in the way that designer tableware might do. The same can be applied to almost any category of object.

FP: Normal is a term that has to do with the idea of conforming to a standard (*norma* = rules in Latin). Super Normal could be taken as meaning something that goes beyond the rules (if we consider the Latin meaning: *super* = above, beyond) but also as something that is really, really normal, that concentrates all quality on normality, and expresses a kind of extra normality (if we consider the Anglo-Saxon use of super as an adjective). How did the definition of Super Normal come about? How should we interpret the term Super Normal and how did you come up with the idea of formalizing Super Normal by gathering real examples?

NF: "Normal" is the situation where something has blended comfortably into our lives. One would venture to say that such things are used unconsciously. I understand it as a term that indicates an entity that is integrated into our lifescape. Within this normal is a particularly symbolic archetype that is "really normal," and this is what has been termed "Super Normal." Super Normal is the normal within the normal.

Jasper and I started collecting things without really talking over beforehand what kinds of things Super Normal defined. I gathered together a lot of things using my own criteria; when I showed these to Jasper, our agreement as to them being Super Normal was almost total. And I agreed completely with all the things Jasper had chosen. Those things at the center of normal may be termed "standard," but when people choose a particular item, I believe that they choose something that is the very epitome of that item. And I believe it's because people know that that's the thing that feels right, that doesn't make waves in their lives. By gathering together and showing these things, we hoped to discover their focal point.

JM: I guess we are talking about the modern sense of the term. I like Francesca's description of concentrating all quality on normality, because I think that within what could be described as normal form or normal character in objects, there are enormous possibilities for creating things that are positive influences on the man-made environment. The term itself can be used various ways. An object can be Super Normal by being so extremely normal that its presence is taken entirely for granted, or it can take its influence from normality and seek to go beyond it by "concentrating all quality on normality," a kind of distilled, concentrated form of normality or summary of everyone's expectations of an object. As for the exhibition and why we decided to do it, it was a natural way to visualize something that at first was rather a vague notion. We knew that Super Normal existed in different guises and gathering together examples was the easiest and most direct way of understanding it. Proposing different objects to each other became a 3-dimensional dialogue before we put any words to it, like two aliens in outer space finding a way to communicate!

FP: What place does Super Normal occupy in your work as designers?

NF: When I start a project these days, I tend to check what is normal or archetypal in the category, because I believe that Super Normal is about extracting the essence of this normality. Once the archetypal character of the category is discovered, I refine it to suit today's lifestyle. This may only involve very slight changes, but I think that when the essence of normal is found and refined, the result is naturally something Super Normal. I try to avoid the pressures of trying to create something new and better, ignoring existing perfections in a category.

JM: Once you notice something Super Normal it becomes a bit of an obsession, it occupies a lot of time. I find myself asking if a thing seems Super Normal before buying it, or comparing two models of a product to decide which might be more Super Normal, or sitting in restaurants turning plates upside down. These moments have always been an important part of how I design and at the start of a project I've noticed myself asking whether it's appropriate to aim for a Super Normal result, but I think an awareness of Super Normal can only be good for one's design. I think most designers get inspiration from looking at life, and this is no different; it's just concentrated on normality.

FP: Why did you feel the need at this point in your careers to develop an idea like Super Normal? Where does this attempt at theorizing come from? Does Super Normal express a reaction against someone or something? And if so, against what?

NF: Whenever I evaluate an object or when I ask myself what part of a design I don't like, I always get hung up on the creator's intentions or the self-expression being at odds with the functions or the harmony inherent in that object. I don't like this aspect of the designs of others and I try to ensure that such things don't appear in my own designs. The idea of designs that result when we take ourselves a little less seriously and do what comes naturally overlaps with Super Normal. I think this comes from a desire to share the pleasurable sensation that comes with realizing the hint of "goodness" in an object that is sensed with the entire body, apart from one's consciousness.

Perhaps both Jasper and myself were tired of the same thing, of designs that are "designed." Perhaps we both felt some kind of intense appeal in things in our daily lives that were not designed, the kind of things that in a certain sense could be called unstylish. Both the "Déjà-vu" stool that I designed for Magis and the cutlery Jasper designed for Alessi are things that play on the feeling cultivated in day to day life. Re-designing something that was normal to start with: that is exactly what the term "Super Normal" expressed. Takashi Okutani came up with the term "Super Normal" when Jasper was talking to him about the cutlery and the "Déjà-vu" stool; I think Jasper was jubilant to have a single term that so precisely expressed his thoughts and feelings. At that moment, the thought took on a concrete form.

It's true that it is a backlash against the kind of design that creates things that do not blend in with people, with the environment and circumstances, or with lifestyles. But it's not a backlash that manifests itself in our movement; I believe that it is a backlash by consumers themselves with respect to their own penchant for a jolt to the senses, when they wake up having found a new feeling of comfort in something, when they realize that what they have been looking for so far are designs that pack a punch. But the punch I'm talking about here is the kind that far exceeds what's required in an object, and it goes without saying that it's necessary only where a design would be inadequate without it.

JM: For me it is a reaction, a reaction to noticing how much better most normal things are than most design things. I think design is in danger of becoming something false and out of tune with real life, when it could be doing something worthwhile. It's degenerating into a marketing tool to promote the identity of companies and to sell magazines. That's not the profession I admired as a student. There's lots of good design going on, maybe more than when I was a student, but unfortunately it's heavily outweighed by what can only be described as visual pollution, atmospheric interference, designs with nothing more in mind than getting noticed, and on balance I'd have to say we would be better off without it. Super Normal is a reminder of more genuine motives for designing something.

FP: Is Super Normal related to your personal idea of beauty? I think it would be interesting to understand your personal point of view on beauty. What is beauty for you in an object? What is a beautiful object?

NF: Beauty can refer to form or shape, but in this case we're thinking in terms of the beauty of the relationship between people, the environment, and circumstances. In other words it's the echo of beauty that arises when we use something. Because the beauty of this relationship lies in the fact that people often use things in similar ways, in similar environments, and under similar circumstances. The beauty of the relationship is therefore naturally narrowed down to certain situations. For example, the way everyone holds the soy sauce dispenser when pouring is the same, and the action of pouring has become part of the atmosphere of enjoying sushi, so that a newer design most likely would not be able to recreate this atmosphere. I think that this beauty arises with the natural, unconscious use of something.

JM: I think Super Normal is wrapped up in a debate about beauty, not just beauty quickly perceived but beauty on other levels, the beauty which takes time to be noticed, which may become beautiful through use, the beauty of the everyday, the beauty of the ugly and the useful, long-term beauty. A beautiful object is not necessarily one with the best shape, and an object may start out ugly and become beautiful over time. Sometimes I'm struck by something beautiful; I buy it, thinking it'll be useful, and discover later on that it never got used and it doesn't seem so beautiful anymore. Actually I think beauty is over-rated.

FP: Jasper, Enzo Mari suggests that the most important thing you did, from a theoretical point of view—the one that best conveyed your personal design philosophy—is the volume *A World Without Words*. Compared to *A World Without Words*, what does Super Normal represent? What is the relationship between the two? And what leads you today to feel the need to formalize your thought with words?

JM: Before it became a book, "A World without Words" was a slide show lecture, a collection of images which meant something to me, put together to get around the difficulty of speaking in public, and perhaps to show that some things don't need to be said. Super Normal could also have been left unsaid but I think there's a lack of discourse in the design world, a kind of noisy silence in which we have all been working. Something had to be said. It probably bothers some people that we're saying it, but I believe Super Normal is a way out of the hole that design has got itself into. There may be other ways, or maybe some people prefer to stay in the hole, but for anyone who cares about it, I hope it will lead to a better understanding of what makes a good object.

FP: I have the impression that Super Normal is essentially confused or taken as a "call to order" regarding the proliferation of signs and forms that produce the visual pollution that surrounds us. On one hand it has been perceived as a Calvinistic stance with respect to homogenized forms and, on the other, as an excess of narcissistic expression. Furthermore, I think the most interesting aspect is the one related to the perception of form vis-à-vis use, which is related to your contesting the prevalence of seeing over the other senses that are more directly involved in the use of an object. What do you think about that?

JM: In the 70s design was all about function, but it was the function of the moment, the kind of function you test while opening a can of peas, asking yourself in that moment how good the can opener is. These days we take function for granted and for the most part things work well enough not to complain about them. So taking a purely functional approach to design would be disastrous. Super Normal's about how things work in relation to our living with them. Not just in one-off use but interactively, over the long term, in relation to everything else we own and use and the atmospheric influence all these things have on our lives. It's interesting to discover, after five years of using a chopping board, that we've been making use of aspects of its design without even noticing them. The slightly curved profile of its sides, which helps us pick it up and stops the wood grain absorbing water while it dries upright on the kitchen counter, and beyond this realization, the sudden appreciation of a form so subtly adapted to its job as to be almost invisibly integrated into the object, allowing it to perform naturally and without any call for praise until we are ready to notice it... I'm getting carried away, but what I mean to say is this discovery is a real wake-up call for what we think of as design. There are levels of sophistication in the object world, achieved most often through the evolutionary forces of an object's development, which make our attempts at design laughable. We can learn a lot from them.

FP: Can you explain your personal relationship to objects? What kind of relationship do you normally establish with the objects that are part of your daily life?

NF: A great deal of our time is taken up with the job of designing, constantly attempting to seek the existence and the shape of things that can be in harmony with, and appropriate for our lives. Within the profusion of signs and forms that get designed there are occasions when we discover the existence of something that gives us a feeling of comfort, something Super Normal. By evaluating the necessity, the appropriateness of a thing's existence in this world, we may discover an intense appeal in an object, which may at first have seemed ugly. I believe that the emotion we feel when we come into contact with the essence of such useful beauty is stronger than the emotion we may feel when we look at something that has been "designed".

JM: I have to confess to being quite obsessive about objects. They are the main subject of my work and occupy a good deal of my day, either in planning them or in studying them. The studying part is all about seeing how they fit in with everything else, what kind of atmospheric influence they have, how they work and how well they work. When coming across a well-balanced object that does everything it should do, it seems to me that it possesses something more than the sum of its parts, a kind of completeness that qualifies it as Super Normal.

FP: In our relationship with objects we are all used to thinking in terms of use, value, and function. However, I recall that some time ago you spoke about a kind of "psychoanalysis of objects," meaning that they could be considered to have a kind of personality, or "objectality," as you called it. Could your research on Super Normal be considered the ongoing development of that idea? And how does it relate to your previous research?

JM: Objectality may have been the first noticing of something Super Normal in objects. I guess you can break down our perception of objects as follows: the first encounter may well be based more on an evaluation of the object's cost, the quality of the object relating to the cost, the perceived usefulness of the object to us, and the object's desirability. But later on, when it comes to living with an object, we forget all about the cost and we have in mind the object's usefulness in relation to certain tasks, how much we enjoy using it, and how much we appreciate it as a possession. It becomes a part of our lives, which we may not think about much but which nevertheless exists, as witnessed when we move house and may be forced to confront the relationship we have with the object in deciding whether to keep it or not. I think this is true no matter how many objects we possess. I remember seeing Gandhi's worldly possessions laid out in the room he occupied in Ahmedabad: a pair of spectacles, a rice bowl, and a piece of cloth, I think that was about it, but it was obvious, thinking about it now, that these objects were Super Normal to him and he needed no others.

FP: Super Normal seems to suggest that objects may be endowed with their own soul, rather than being inanimate objects. This perspective is probably closer to Japanese culture and its world populated by a divine being, connected to the presences of the Kami. What do you think?

NF: There is a kind of beauty, a purity to brand-new objects that have been untouched by human hands. In the Shinto faith, there is a philosophy that links the beauty of such untouched objects to God and that searches for a beauty removed from those things tainted by the real world in which we live, this being the world of God. Another idea is that an implement that has been newly created and not yet used has no soul. In contrast, something used by many people (this doesn't mean just one item; it means a number of the same implements used by many) has a soul to it. Through many people using it, an object is substantiated and attains a brilliance; the weight of the soul within this object shows its worth. *Wabi-sabi* is a beauty that arises after useful beauty has been mastered.

FP: I recently read an article in an old issue of *Domus*, written by Yusaku Kamekura (a graphic designer and a pioneer of modernity in postwar Japan) about form and tradition in Japan. He talks about the concept of "pure" form—form that is not subject to market pressures or any other pressure—using the term *katachi*, a quality expressing a particular aspect of form, connected to a specific emotional and rational quality. He writes: "a form that is present both in the matter and in the action..." and "In Japan form still expresses simplicity, elegance and splendor..." and "I think it is of the utmost importance to fight against what is possible and achieve the impossible. "

NF: I believe that in Japan, there is a tendency to take the actual act of using a thing as beauty. This is precisely the beauty of the relationship between objects and people. For example, a chair might have a backrest with a shape that invites me to lean on it when I'm standing behind it, so it's not the beauty of the shape as such that is appreciated but rather a form's presence that sparks off actions and contributes to the atmosphere around it. A form that beautifies behavior and actions, or a form that beautifies the relationship between itself and the things around it, has to be something that does not fix action and environment, but something you might call a generic, overall beauty that grants a degree of freedom. So there is a tendency towards objects inevitably taking on a simplicity. Or there is a tendency for things to become easier to use function-wise. I believe that representations of

decorativeness or ornateness for the sake of appreciation
are far-removed and separate from useful beauty.

**FP: I don't really understand the deep meaning or the
significance of this culture of form, but I would like to understand, Naoto, how you relate to that tradition. More generally,
how does your idea of Super Normal relate respectively to
good design and the Modern, on one hand and the Japanese,
on the other–both implicitly referring to an idea of simplicity
and formal clarity?**

NF: I think that beauty of function is the kind of beauty where all
attention is focused on the function of an object, instead of forms
with decorative or ornamental nuances or expressions. And any
expression of self on the part of the creator is also done away
with; by focusing on function, any emotion that may be attached
to an object and its uses is eliminated, and the object can thus
fulfill its function perfectly. That's the way I see it. It's like people
being respected for getting down to it and focusing on their own
particular role, so that an unseen yet cohesive relationship is built
up. It's the same with objects: a focus on function and a lack of
emotion in the equation means that our connection to the object
becomes more attractive and we develop an affinity for it. In a
sense, it's where an object is perfect and uncompromising in
function, even though it is modest and doesn't make a personal
statement. A relationship where there is no flattery on either
side is the base of the Japanese aesthetic consciousness. But
focusing on function also means that objects allow us to use
them in many different ways. Instead of a hammer whose rubber
grip has four grooves for fingers molded into it, one with a simple,
easy-to-use round wooden handle is a form that comes to feel
comfortable in one's hand, as its shape changes slowly with use;
it's one that has a lot of freedom to it and can be used when
hammering in any type of nail. Like a hammer, we're talking about
objects that don't advertise "Hey, I'm easy to use" just with
their shape. Super Normal refers exactly to that simple, straight-
forward hammer icon.

**FP: The selection of Super Normal objects comprises objects
of known authors (for example, world famous designers like
Sori Yanagi, Enzo Mari, and Konstantin Grcic) and anonymous,
everyday products without specific aesthetic intent. What
do they share that makes them all Super Normal?**

NF: There is a feeling of comfort in using anonymous things that
have been around for a long time. Out-living other things, which
proved less enduring, they have become so familiar to us
that we rarely ask ourselves who their creator might have been.

Designers often hold the greatest respect for such objects, aware of the undeniable beauty within these normal things. They frequently derive great inspiration from them. The Super Normal that already existed and the Super Normal that has been achieved more recently have a unified value; the only difference is how long they have been used and the presence or absence of the creator's name.

JM: I couldn't say it any better than that, except to add that what unites the two categories may be a motivation to put the object ahead of the individual creative ego as opposed to the urge to have it noticed. The evolutionary step instead of the creative leap. Not that a Super Normal object is uncreative, but the creativity is less focused on the visual aspect of an object's character and more on creating an object in balance with its role and with its likely environment.

FP: I believe that the goose egg, especially if compared to the chicken egg we are all more familiar with, seems to be the form allowing us to immediately understand the concept of Super Normal. This idea of a slight deviation from the standard—a mini-mal intervention that acts as a shift in meaning—is one of the concepts that clearly emerges from both Super Normal and your activity in general. I am thinking for example about Jasper's Glo Ball; in this lamp the deviation from the pure geometrical shape is evident. Can you tell us something more about this? Are there other Super Normal objects that could be perceived in terms of this perspective?

JM: The minimal intervention or subtle change could be a change of scale or proportion, just as it could be a slight simplification or the adaptation of a successful feature of an object to a new form, or the concentration of an object's character. Many of the exhibits are examples of these possibilities and I agree that the goose egg demonstrates this very well. Some other obvious ones are N° 1, the tables on which everything is displayed (designed by Jean Nouvel); N° 21, Enzo Mari's Mariolina chair; N° 118, the paper clip; N° 166, Fiskar scissors; and N° 205, the Herald Tribune newspaper.

FP: Some anonymous Japanese objects can be found in the exhibition, such as the salt cellar from the Japanese state monopoly. This object is obviously experienced in a different way by Naoto and Jasper. For Naoto it probably belongs to his memory/history. To what extent does the history of an object effect the way it is perceived when used? What is the impact of the history of an object or of its author's personality on the way it is perceived when used?

JM: I think there's a sub-group of Super Normal objects, which is a very subjective one. They are Super Normal through familiarity and even nostalgic memories. I think everyone could point to at least one item in their home and describe it as an object they love to have around for the memory of past atmosphere that it evokes. Our appreciation of atmosphere is often linked or cross-referenced with the past and objects that played a part in some previous atmospheric memories have a powerful hold on us. For me N° 29 bicycle handlebars could easily be included in this category, as my first serious bicycle had very similar ones, or N° 203 Alvar Aalto stool, which a childhood friend had at his house.

FP: All the objects in your selection—whether designed or anonymous, of eastern or western origins, modern or contemporary—show a common spirit, and I really appreciate that. Nowadays, many people talk about the risks connected to cultural homogeneity and globalization; your exhibition is a selection of industrial objects mirroring some aspects of a consistency that can not be clearly explained but that can be clearly seen in practice. Do you think Super Normal can be considered as a catalogue of examples of a possible idea of modernity shared by the East and the West? Can Super Normal be generally considered as a rejection of the "design style"?

JM: I hadn't thought of it before, but now you mention it, I can see it as a kind of spirit of things, which is both modern and old fashioned and which I think could be understood by anyone. They might not all be everyone's idea of good taste, but then they are not objects that need to be judged in terms of taste. I think they represent an advanced level of object precisely because they reject design as an issue of taste.

FP: Is what I heard about Sori Yanagi true, about his visiting the exhibition in Tokyo and asking who had designed an object that he forgot he'd designed many years before? That would be extraordinary evidence of the detachment from one's ego as an author. However, it also suggests that the object has achieved that specific level of sophistication mentioned by Jasper. Jasper states that objects achieve a consistent shape after a formal process of adjustment that can only be appraised on the long term and that results from the efforts of many designers—often anonymous—over time.

NF: Through the years, objects are created and then used; any deficiencies are corrected; the object is used again … then corrected again—the relationship between people and objects reaches an end point. This also means that the form reaches an end form. This does not mean that designers picked out this end form, but rather that the shape has resulted from the use of that object in day-to-day life by many people and over time. Who designed the object is no longer that important. If a designer believes that people and time have created a form, then they want to get rid of the ego that says, "I designed this object"–I think this is a modest, natural turn of events. Like the flow of water or the wind smoothing the edges of rocks so they take on a roundness. When people use something that leads to a particular form, the result is something normal. The end point of this is Super Normal.

FP: It seems that some designers have been able to interfere in that process of evolution and give a positive shift to it. For instance, Enzo Mari says that the designer is the guardian of a collective knowledge and that the project often "involves the slight adjustment of details, because the structural functionality of objects has been regulated by ancient use."

JM: I think he's quite right although the amount of shift may vary. I like the idea that we are guardians of a collective knowledge, and the passing on of it could be seen as a parallel to the evolutionary process, whereby things that don't work are discarded and things that do work are built upon. Looking at the development of objects from the first tool until recently, this has been the case, but the modern creative urge in humankind is strong enough to override this commonsense approach, even though in most cases the result is a failure. The entertainment provided by these formal gymnastics seems to be enough to justify the exercise. The bigger the shift that Enzo Mari speaks of, the less likely it is to stick.

FP: Naoto mentioned the *wabi-sabi* principle, which implies an idea of beauty or serenity that comes with age, when the life of the object is evidenced in its patina and wear, or in any visible repairs. With the concept of Super Normal you are suggesting that the use is a relation that strengthens over time. You also mentioned a kind of relation to the objects that does not necessarily involve the fact that an object is "nice" (Naoto speaks about the "beauty of the ugly"). How do aspects of imperfection or use-dependent transformation of the material state of the object contribute to the definition of a Super Normal quality?

NF: In Japan, we have the word *shutaku*. A literal translation would be "polished by hand." It is a metaphor for something that's been used and become better after having been touched again and again; *shutaku* is a polished luster; it is also a metaphor for something that has taken on a personality of its own, or improved with age. It fits comfortably in one's hand, a metaphor for something that has come to fit in our lifestyle. This same meaning is included in *wabi* and *sabi*, but the awkward beauty of something decaying over time indicates an overall beauty, which human hands cannot touch directly; nature in its entirety has weathered that thing. *Shutaku* expresses the beauty that occurs with time when an object survives constant use, undergoes a metamorphosis and becomes more beautiful than something that is new. It's talking about the deepening of a relationship. Something that isn't found in an object that graces a shelf; the form and luster an object gains as people use it deepens its beauty: it invites people to get attached to it.

So both *shutaku* and *wabi-sabi* refer to things that aren't cool design-wise but rather normal which nothing special about them except that they have the potential for becoming great with use. Something that was normal gains *shutaku* and has the potential for acquiring the beauty of *wabi-sabi*. That's because with something that has been created not with beauty but with function in mind, this modesty becomes even more *wabi* and *sabi*.

Super Normal means things that move towards this normal – it's talking about awkward beauty.

JM: That sums up the physical side of Super Normal very well, and I'd only add that I think there is also a less physical transformation that objects we possess go through with time. For example, the accumulated use of a hammer or a teapot (separately, of course) creates a relationship between user and object which may be parallel to its material change but never theless independent. We come to appreciate an object through using it, and the more we use a good object, the more we are able to appreciate its qualities, and we may discover its beauty not just in how it ages but in how we age with it.

Francesca Picchi is an architect and editor of the Italian magazine, *Domus*. She was visiting professor of design history at Politecnico di Milano's design school. Her curatorial work includes *Enzo Mari: il lavoro al centro* (Barcelona, 1999), *The View From Domus. Fotografie/Photographs 1928–2002* (Milan, 2002), and *Kuramata's Tokyo* (Milan, 2003). She lives and works in Milan.

Naoto Fukosawa

Born in Yamanashi, Japan, in 1956. Graduated from Tama Art
University in 1980. Joined Seiko Epson, engaged in the advanced
design of watches and other micro-electronics. In 1989, joined
the San Francisco product design firm ID TWO, the predecessor
to IDEO. In 1996, returned to Japan to start and head up IDEO's
Tokyo office. In 2003, established Naoto Fukasawa Design.
Since 2001, a design advisory board member for MUJI. In 2003,
launched ±0 (PLUS MINUS ZERO brand). Designs for B&B ITALIA,
Driade, Magis, Artemide, Danese, Boffi and other European
and Japanese clients.

Jasper Morrison

Born in London in 1959. Studied at Kingston Polytechnic,
London, Hochschule der Künste, Berlin, and Royal College of Art,
London. Established Office for Design in London in 1986.
Designs for a number of leading manufacturers in Europe and
Asia, including Alessi, Cappellini, Flos, Magis, Muji, Samsung&Vitra.
Represented by Galerie Kreo in Paris. Jasper Morrison Ltd. has
offices in London, Paris, and Tokyo.

1	Wastepaper basket "in attesa" 1971 Enzo Mari Danese, Italy polypropylene		11	Chair "Mariolina" 2002 Enzo Mari Magis, Italy steel in epoxy resin, polypropylene	
2	Small chair 2005 Naoto Fukasawa Maruni Wood Industry, Japan beech		12	Ashtray Noritake, Japan melamine	
3	Citrus basket 370 1952 Ufficio technico Alessi, Italy stainless steel		13	"Uni-tray" 1976 1999 Riki Watanabe Sato Shoji Stainless steel	
4	"Smokey joe" silver charcoal grill Weber, USA steel, Alminium		14	"Canary" sandals Nishibe Chemical, Japan	
5	Air filter 2003 Muji, Japan		15	Goose egg	
6	Square brush washer Japan ceramics		16	Calculator 2004 Muji, Japan aluminium	
7	Bathroom stool 1990 Marna, Japan polypropylene		17	Ashtray 2003 Muji, Japan porcelain	
8	Bucket Italy plastic		18	Bottle opener "Stavros" 1999 Marc Newson Alessi, Italy stainless steel, plastic	
9	Basket Cyunichi Jyuki, Japan polypropylene		19	Stools "Déjà-vu" 2005 Naoto Fukasawa Magis, Italy aluminium	
10	Bicycle 2005 Muji, Japan		20	Cocktail shaker 870 1957 Carlo Mazzeri/Luigi Massoni Alessi, Italy stainless steel	

21	Sieve Ikeda Plastic Sales, Japan polypropylene		

22	Ice bucket 871 1957 Carlo Mazzeri/Luigi Massoni Alessi, Italy stainless steel		

23	Fiber-tipped pen Pentel, Japan recycled polypropylene, recycled polyethylene		

24	Package-carrier handle Japan polypropylene		

25	Wastebin "Trash" 2005 Jasper Morrison Magis, Italy polypropylene		

26	"Less" 1994 Jean Nouvel Unifor, Italy steel		

27	Coat stand "Hut ab" 1998 Konstantin Grcic Nils Holger Moormann, Germany ash		

28	Sake glass 1976 Sori Yanagi Toyo Sasaki Glass, Japan glass		

29	"G type" soy sauce dispenser 1958 Masahiro Mori Hakusan Porcelain, Japan porcelain		

30	Table salt shaker The Salt Industry Center of Japan glass, polypropylene and polyethylene		

31	Pepper mill 76 1965 Carlo Mazzeri/Anselmo Vitale Alessi, Italy stainless steel		

32	Sugar sifter 70 1962 Carlo Mazzeri/Anselmo Vitale Alessi, Italy stainless steel		

33	Gem clip Norica, Germany		

34	"GR digital" camera 2005 Masahiro Kurita/Tatsuo Okuda, Ricoh, Japan diecast magnesium		

35	NT cutter NT Cutter, Japan ABS plastic, polyoxymethylene		

36	Tall tea cup 2004 Muji, Japan porcelain		

37	Ice cream spoon circa 2000 Sori Yanagi Sato Shoji, Japan stainless steel		

38	Thermometer Empex Instruments, Japan wood, glass		

39	Flour scoop stainless		

40	Bowl stainless steel		

41	Vermilion calligraphy ink	
	Kaimei, Japan	
	polyethylene	

42	"Yamato" library paste bottle	
	Yamato, Japan	
	body: recycled polyethylene cap: polyethylen	

43	Salt caster/Spice holder "Zenit"	
	2002	
	Marc Newson	
	Alessi, Italy	
	crystal glass, stainless steel	

44	Bar sugar bowl 50/55	
	1961/1964	
	Carlo Mazzeri/Anselmo Vitale	
	Alessi, Italy	
	stainless steel	

45	Grill pan	
	2002	
	Sori Yanagi	
	Sato Shoji, Japan	
	cast iron	

46	Milk bottle	
	circa 1965	
	TOYO Glass, Japan	
	glass	

47	Tumbler	
	Toyo Sasaki Glass, Japan	
	tempered glass	

48	Wine glass	
	glass	

49	Door handle	
	1990	
	Jasper Morrison	
	FSB, Germany	
	cast aluminium	

50	"REX" peeler	
	1947	
	Alfred Neweczersal	
	Zena, Switzerland	
	aluminium handle and stainless steel	

51	Spanners	
	MBPerraud outillage, France	
	Chromed forged steel	

52	Felt undershoes	
	Germany	
	Felt	

53	Shelf unit	
	2003	
	Muji, Japan	
	pine	

54	DVD/MD stereo component	
	Naoto Fukasawa	
	Plusminuszero, Japan	

55	Tea canister	
	Tomita Press Industry, Japan	
	stainless steel	

56	Tea canister	
	Kaikado, Japan	
	tin	

57	Shelf light "Wenig"	
	2004	
	Klaus Hackl	
	Nils Holger Moormann, Germany	
	alminium	

58	Melamine tableware	
	Noritake, Japan	
	melamine	

59	Melamine tableware	
	Noritake, Japan	
	melamine	

60	Hammered teapot chased teapot	
	Akao Aluminium, Japan	
	aluminium	

61	Kettle 2005 Muji, Japan stainless steel	71	Paper weight with loupe "TV" 2006 Naoto Fukasawa B & B Italia, Italy solid glass
62	Stainless steel clothes pin Ohki Seisakusyo, Japan stainless steel	72	Handlebar Switzerland aluminium
63	Ashtray Japan stainless steel	73	Pocket-size stapler 2004 Muji, Japan
64	Bucket Japan galvanised sheet steel	74	Knife sharpener Robert Welch, UK steel
65	Water ladle Iguma Seisakusyo, Japan stainless steel, beech	75	"Tin family" 1998 Jasper Morrison Alessi, Italy stainless steel
66	Table "Atlas" System 1992 Jasper Morrison for Alias, Italy steel swaged tube, aluminium, laminate tops and cast aluminium bases	76	"Konstantin Grcic goblet" Konstantin Grcic Iittala, Finland glass
67	Sugar bowl 1967 Arne Jacobsen Stelton, Denmark stainless steel	77	Joint tap 2006 Muji, Japan
68	Dual-grit rubber semi-rough/rough Lion Office Products, Japan used paper, natural rubber	78	VLM switch 1968 Achille Castiglioni VLM, Italy
69	Coin tray Japan	79	Egg carton molded paper kenaf, reed
70	"Tolomeo" desk lamp 1986 Giancarlo Fassina/Michele de Lucchi Artemide, Italy aluminium	80	Electric thermos kettle Naoto Fukasawa Plusminuszero, Japan

| 81 | "Striped" chair
 2005
 Ronan & Erwan Bouroullec
 Magis, Italy <br> steel | | 91 | Stainless steel bowl, strainer
 1960/1999
 Sori Yanagi
 Sato Shoji, Japan <br> stainless steel | |

81   "Striped" chair
2005
Ronan & Erwan Bouroullec
Magis, Italy
steel

82   "Wave" music sytem
2005

Bose, USA

83   Chopping board

Japan
Wood

84   Round tray JM14/Small bowl JM15/16/17/Ashtray JM18
2002
Jasper Morrison
Alessi, Italy
stainless steel

85   Universal Shelving System 606 (photo)
1960
Dieter Rams
Vitsoe, UK
aluminium, steel, fibreboard and beech veneer

86   Rice bowl
2004

Muji, Japan
porcelain

87   Decanter
2004
Antonio Citterio/Toan Nguyen
Iittala, Finland
hand-blown glass

88   Can opener

Kobo Aizawa, Japan
stainless steel

89   Serving plates JM13
2000
Jasper Morrison
Alessi, Italy
stainless steel

90   "Moon" dining plate, tea cup, tea pot
1997
Jasper Morrison
Rosenthal, Germany
porcelain

91   Stainless steel bowl, strainer
1960/1999
Sori Yanagi
Sato Shoji, Japan
stainless steel

92   Sake sampling cup

Japan
porcelain

93   Rectangular plate
2004

Muji, Japan
porcelain

94   Round stool

Houtoku, Japan
polyethylene, chrome plated steel

95   Wine and beer glasses
1979/1970
Sori Yanagi
Sato Shoji, Japan
glass

96   "Op-La" tray-table
1998
Jasper Morrison
Alessi, Italy
stainless steel , ABS plastic

97   Glass

glass

98   Coffeemaker "Moka express"
1950's

Bialetti, Italy
aluminium

99   Ice cream spoon

Japan
wood

100   Paper coaster

Sakura napkin, Japan
paper

101 Hanging lamp "Glo-Ball" 1999 Jasper Morrison Flos, Italy glass	111 "Penguin" soy sauce dispenser Shinki Gosei, Japan polyethylene, acrylonitrile butadiene styrene
102 Water pitcher Ebematsu, Japan polycarbonate	112 Salad dressing pour-bottle Japan PET
103 "neon" mobile telephone 2005 Naoto Fukasawa au KDDI, Japan	113 Pencil sharpner DUX, Germany glass
104 "FRISK" mint (packaging) Perfetti Van Melle, Belgium ABS plastic	114 Liquitex "Gesso" Liquitex, USA polypropylene, polyethelene
105 "Kono" drip-coffeer set 2005 Coffee Syphon, Japan glass	115 Ashtray "Cubo" 1957 Bruno Munari Danese, Italy melamine, alminium
106 Extrafine ballpoint pen Mitsubishipencil, Japan PVC	116 Ball Japan plastic
107 Magazine-format notepad 2003 Muji, Japan recycled paper	117 Folding "Air-Chair" 2001 Jasper Morrison Magis, Italy fibreglass-reinforced polypropylene
108 "Flores" box 1991 Enzo Mari Danese, Italy Thermoplastic polymer	118 Washing-up brush Coronet, Germany Wood, polypropylene
109 Ceiling lamp "Akari" 1951 Isamu Noguchi Ozeki, Japan handmade washi paper and bamboo ribbing	119 Mesh tarp tote bag 2005 Naoto Fukasawa Plusminuszero, Japan PET
110 Tool box Trusco Nakayama, Japan steel	120 Luxo L1 lamp 1937 Jac Jacobsen Luxo ASA, Norway Steel

121	Fabric bags		131	Ruled notepads
				2006
	Muji, Japan			Muji, Japan
	cotton			recycled paper

121 Fabric bags

Muji, Japan
cotton

122 Floor lamp "Glo-Ball"
1999
Jasper Morrison
Flos, Italy
glass

123 Dessert glass

Toyo Sasaki Glass, Japan
glass

124 Oven toaster

Naoto Fukasawa
Plusminuszero, Japan

125 Measuring tape
2004

Muji, Japan
steel

126 Coat hanger

wire

127 "Mellina" tray

Toshiyuki Kita
Kokusai Kako, Japan
melamine

128 Half-pint glass

UK
glass

129 Melamin facial tissue box

Shohei Mihara
Threeline, Japan
melamin

130 Funnel

aluminium

131 Ruled notepads
2006

Muji, Japan
recycled paper

132 Bic Biro pen

Bic, France

133 Wrist watch "Databank tele memo 30"

Casio computer, Japan
glass, stainless steel

134 Salad bowls 205
1967
Carlo Mazzeri/Anselmo Vitale
Alessi, Italy
stainless steel

135 Magnifying glass

Niigata seiki, Japan
glass

136 Tongs

Stainless steel

137 "Scotch" transparent adhesive tape

3 M, USA
polypropylene

128 Eraser (white/black)
2005

Muji, Japan
Rubber

139 Palette knife
1966

Kawashima Industry, Japan
stainless steel, wood

140 "Merci" coloured rubber bands

Kantoushizai, Japan
rubber

141 Cigarette lighter Bic

Bic, France

142 Household cutter

Stanley

143 Art work cutter

Stanley

144 Notepad with cover

Rhodia, France
paper

145 Oil painting brush

Holbein Art Materials, Japan
mongoose fur

146 "Cotman" water colours

Winsor & Newton, UK

147 "Sakura" three-cup brush washer

Sakura Color Products, Japan

148 "Air-Chair"
1999
Jasper Morrison
Magis, Italy
fibreglass-reinforced polypropylene

149 Ballpoint pen (oil-based ink)
2006

Muji, Japan
ABS polycarbonated

150 Lightweight wall hook

Gorikiisland, Japan
brass

151 Portable MD player
2006
Naoto Fukasawa
Plusminuszero, Japan

152 "Choro Q" toy car

Tomy, Japan
ABS plastic, synthetic rubber

153 Palette knife (size 850, size 868)

Jack Richeson & Co., USA

154 Table alarm clock "Optic"
1970 (1988)
Joe Colombo
Alessi, Italy
ABS plastic, quartz movement.

155 Mortar and pestle

ceramic

156 Bulldog clip

plastic

157 Round name plate

Mammoth, Japan
recycled plastic

158 Server spoon & fork
1974
Sori Yanagi
Sato Shoji, Japan
stainless steel

159 Ladle

Akao Aluminium, Japan
aluminium

160 Dipping sauce cup

Muji, Japan
porcelain

161　Japanese tea cup
2004

Muji, Japan
porcelain

162　Cafe table

D&DEPARTMENT, Japan
melamine, steel

163　Sim Chair
1999
Jasper Morrison
Vitra, Switzerland
polypropylene, chromed steel

164　Wall clock
1956
Max Bill
Junghans, Germany
aluminium, glass and quartz movement

165　"Tenjin" chalk case

Nihon Tenjin Hakuboku Kogyo, Japan

166　Package-carrier handle

Japan
polypropylene

167　Cutlery tray "ABC"
1996
Jasper Morrison
Magis, Italy.
polypropylene

168　"KnifeForkSpoon" cutlery set
2004
Jasper Morrison
Alessi, Italy
Stainless steel

169　Rosti "Margrethe" bowl
1954
Sigvard Bernadotte / Acton Bjorn
Rosti, Denmark
melamine

170　Measuring cup

Arcoroc, France
heat resistant glass

171　"Rollfix" measuring tape

Hoechstmass, Germany
ABS plastic

182　Inkpads
2006
Naoto Fukasawa
Shachihata, Japan
recycled PBT, PET and PE plastics

173　Colour-coded draughting scale

Sanko Drawing Instruments, Japan
recycled ABS plastic

174　"Easy cellular phone S A101K"
2005
Shinya Kosai
Kyocera, Japan
polycarbonate

175　Scissors
1970's

Fiskars, Finland
polyurethan and stainless steel

176　"Amami" lamp
2006
Naoto Fukasawa
Danese, Italy
polycarbonate

177　Push pin

Moore, USA
Steel point, Aluminium head

178　Plate

Ebematsu, Japan
stainless steel

179　Melamine tableware

Noritake, Japan
melamine

180　22V LCD TV

Naoto Fukasawa
Plusminuszero, Japan

181 Wrist watch "Grand Seiko"
2003
Toshiro Matsubara
Seiko Watch Corporation, Japan
stainless steel

182 Chair 03
1999
Maarten Van Severen
Vitra, Switzerland
polyurethane foam, steel, aluminium

183 8-inch LCD TV

Naoto Fukasawa

Plusminuszero, Japan

184 Table clock
1956
Angelo Mangiarotti
Klein & More, Germany
ceramics, acryl

185 Coat hanger

Muji, Japan
polypropylene

186 Tray table "Mate"
1992
Achille Castiglioni
de Padova, Italy
tray: benchwood, base: cotton

187 Drinking glasses SG 52
2003
Stefano Giovannoni
Alessi, Italy
crystal glass

188 Edo-style soy sauce dispenser

glass

189 Condiment set 5070
1978
Ettore Sottsass
Alessi, Italy
stainless steel and crystal

190 Tray

Naoto Fukasawa
Plusminuszero, Japan
metacrylic

191 Clothe peg

World-plus, Japan
wood

192 Calculator
2004

Muji, Japan
aluminium

193 "Drapas" template

Sanko Drawing Instruments, Japan

194 Paintbrush (size 8)

Namura Taiseido, Japan

195 Round partitioned plate
2005

Muji, Japan
porcelain

196 Vegetable brush

Japan

197 Tray 5006
1982
Ettore Sottsass
Alessi, Italy
stainless steel

198 Furniture handle MN1116 "Smooth"
2005
James Irvine
Pamar, Italy
diecast aluminium

199 Spoons

Japan
stainless steel

200 Bottle opener

Kirin, Japan

201 Tray

Stainless steel

---

202 Milk jug

Aoyoshi, Japan

---

203 "Joyn" furniture system (photo)
2002
Ronan and Erwan Bouroullec
Vitra, Switzerland

---

204 Ketchup & mustard containers

polyethylene

---

205 Cutlery set "Nuovo Milano"
1987
Ettore Sottsass/Alberto Gozzi
Alessi, Italy
stainless steel

---

206 3 legs stool
1933
Alvar Aalto
Artek, Finland
Wood

---

207 Parmesan cheese cellar 5071
1978
Ettore Sottsass
Alessi, Italy
stainless steel and crystal

---

208 Herald Tribune

paper

---

209 Cityhall clock
1955
Arne Jacobsen
Mobach, Netherlands
aluminium, glass

---

210 Super Normal book
2007
Naoto Fukasawa/Jasper Morrison
Lars Müller Publishers, Switzerland
Paper

Sori Yanagi suddenly turned up out of the blue during preparations for the Super Normal exhibition held in June 2006 at the AXIS gallery in Tokyo. These photos were taken at that time.

Speaking of Sori Yanagi, it can be said that his design, throughout a long and brilliant career, has always been Super Normal, and this is reflected by the numerous designs of his in the exhibition. It's a great honor for us that, despite his great age, he made this visit to the exhibition.

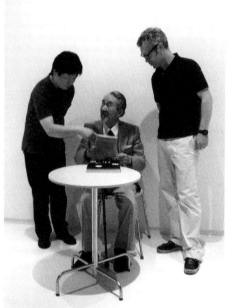

With thanks to:
Simon Alderson, Axis Inc., Stefano Boeri,
Christoph Brach, Andrea Cancellato, Tony Cunningham,
Fumiko Ito, Asami Koga, Laurence Mauderli,
Piero Molteni, Ryu Niimi, Takashi Okutani, Alice Rawsthorn,
Keiko Sano, Catherine Schelbert, Twentytwentyone,
Unifor, Jun Yasumoto

Concept: Jasper Morrison, Naoto Fukasawa, Lars Müller
Production: Integral Lars Müller
Lithography: Jung Crossmedia Publishing, Lahnau
Printing and binding: Graspo, Zlín, the Czech Republic

Translation from Japanese: Mardi Miyake
Copyediting: Catherine Schelbert

Photographs:
Jasper Morrison
MRSmagazine Bunka Publishing Bureau (p. 12–13)
Katrin Paul (p. 19, 30–31, 61 bottom, 73 top, 87 bottom, 93, 94)

©2007/2024 Lars Müller Publishers

Lars Müller Publishers
Zürich, Switzerland
www.lars-mueller-publishers.com

Distributed in North America by ARTBOOK | D.A.P.
www.artbook.com

ISBN 978-3-03778-106-7

Printed in the Czech Republic

Published by Lars Müller Publishers on the occasion
of the exhibition "Super Normal" at the Triennale di Milano,
April 18–23, 2007, during the Salone Internazionale del Mobile.

The exhibition was previously held at the Axis Gallery in Tokyo,
in June 2006, and at twentytwentyone in London,
in September 2006.